Prophetic Guidance
An Earthly Guide to Assist You With Your Heavenly Assignment

Prophetic Guidance
An Earthly Guide to Assist You With Your Heavenly Assignment

Iris L. Jones Ministries/Enterprises, Inc. Publishing -2018

Prophetic Guidance
An Earthly Guide to Assist You With Your Heavenly Assignment
Iris L. Jones

Copyright © 2018 by Iris L. Jones of Iris L. Jones Ministries, Incorporated & Iris L. Jones Enterprises, Incorporated

All scripture quotations, unless otherwise indicated, are taken from the Holy Bible: King James Version, New King James Version, New Living Translation Version, New International Readers Version, English Standard Version, The Living Bible, NET Version, Holman Christian Standard Bible Version, God's Word Version, WEB Version, Parallel Version and The Message Version. Used by permission.

ISBN-13: 978-0692067901 (Iris L. Jones Enterprises, Inc.)

ISBN-10: 0692067906

All rights reserved. No part of this book may be reproduced or transmitted in any form or by any means without written permission from the author.

This book was printed in the United States of America. Cover art created by Flaming Sword Productions, Inc.

All Rights Reserved.

FOREWORD

"My child, you did not purchase this book in vain. I AM The LORD, who covers you and protects you from this day forward as you go forth in ministry. Not only will you prosper but you will live a life of abundance. I have many great things in store for you as you teach My people about My Word and My Kingdom.

Each and every chosen prophet of Mine are to be encouraged from this day forward. You are anointed to win and prosper for I give you the power to get wealth. You will come to understand that spiritual wealth is greater than tangible wealth. You will begin to overstep the boundaries that once banned you from sharing Me with the world. You are now entering your portion of the prophetic Goshen that I have prepared for you and the generations that are birthed through you.

I admonish you to seek sound doctrine and effective prophetic training and development which starts with obeying Me. I will lead you and guide you. If you do not learn to obey Me, you will have a difficult time obeying others. Do not concern yourself with any hindrances that may interfere with your development, for I will surely give you a way of escape and will not put more on you than you can bear.

Continue to seek My Kingdom first. Continue to intercede for the lost souls; there are many that are waiting on you to help them. Continue to pray without ceasing and depend on Me to be your Comfort. You are entering a time of Divine

Restitution and your works will be rewarded for keeping Me first in your life. I have regarded you as a mouthpiece for My nations and many will know you because of your sincere love for Me."

-Inspired by The Pneuma of GOD

ACKNOWLEDGEMENTS

Thank you to each and every prophetic word and declaration of support that was spoken over my life as this book was being birthed. GOD gave me the vision for this book in 2015 after I relocated to an unfamiliar region. Little did I know that this book would serve as a kind of life support for me. It was very difficult to birth this book, just as it is difficult to serve as a Kingdom Prophet when others will try to convince you that you are not obeying GOD. The warfare that comes with new territories and regions are unimaginable but GOD continues to show us true prophets that when HE has an assignment for us to complete, that according to HIS Will it shall be fulfilled.

I want to encourage those who have supported my ministry over the past ten years to continue to trust GOD. I am a living testimony that when you are obedient to HIM, you will be kept and covered by HIS Ruach.

I thank my veteran and new supporters for purchasing this book. Thank you to my spiritual covering Christian International Apostolic Network for teaching me a great deal about the prophetic through your writings and teachings. I am grateful for the prayers and intercessions of those at Christian International Ministries, of Santa Rosa Beach, FL.

I also thank my former mentors and prophetic trainers who have helped me along the way as I have developed as a prophet.

Thank you to my children for believing in my ministry and for encouraging me when I needed it. To all of my family, spiritual affiliations and mentees, thank you for your support and prayers as well.

Iris L. Jones

CONTENTS

I. The Making of a Prophet

II. The Bible is Prophecy

III. Dimensions of the Prophetic

IV. The Prophetic Mantle

V. The Journey of a Prophet

VI. Prophetic Integrity

VII. Who Needs the Prophet, and Who the Prophet Needs

VIII. Prophets and The Church

IX. Prophetic Prayer

X. Reflection

INTRODUCTION

Prophets know in part, and prophesy in part (1 Corinthians 13:9). When the HOLY SPIRIT directed me to write this handbook for the prophets who seek HIM diligently, I did not know where to beg n. I could not rely solely on the 16 plus years of prophetic training that I've received. I had to humbly ask the HOLY SPIRIT for help. This writing is to help those who know who they are in CHRIST JESUS, but need clarity and understanding of the scripture and operations of the prophetic, in order to be an effective prophet.

We are in an era where prophets are arising from the Heavens (spirit), and where prophets are arising from the Earth (flesh). While prophets are instructed by GOD to serve on Earth, there are some who have succumbed to their Heavenly assignment. While their intention is to serve they are hurting many, instead of truthfully assisting Our FATHER in helping HIS people. We must know and discern the difference between them. As a part of the governmental function of the prophetic, GOD entrusted me with the task to edify, exhort and comfort those who want to grow deeper in relationship with JESUS CHRIST, for the testimony of JESUS is the spirit of prophecy (Revelation 19:10).

If your prophetic utterances are not causing the Believer to seek the same JESUS that is within you, then you are not a prophet. Prophets are sent to help the non-believer become a believer. It is the prophet's responsibility to share a word from the HEAVENS that will cause believers and non-believers alike to trust the LORD even more, or once again.

My question to you is what makes you a prophet? Everyone who quotes Jeremiah 1:5 is not a prophet.

Jeremiah, a prophet came to understand that he was ordained by GOD before his mother became impregnated with him. How did he know? *"The word of the LORD came unto him (me), saying..."* (Jeremiah 1:4). My question to you is: How do you know that you were ordained by GOD to be HIS prophet?

I will give you a few possible answers of how to determine if you are a prophet: 1) The revelations that you speak come to pass, 2) You live a holy and separated life unto GOD and 3) you live by HIS words, and those alone. These are just a few indications that you are one; not to overlook the many hardships that you may have endured that only GOD could have delivered you out of.

This book will *not* answer all of the questions that you have about the prophetic. Many must become members of a church that teaches sound doctrine, inclusive of the importance of the prophetic. You must learn the Word of GOD and how to rightfully divide it. You must learn protocol and correct interpretation of the Word of GOD in order to be a successful minister of the Gospel.

Along with appropriate training, this book is a great starting point to learn *who* you are as a *true* prophet. It is my hope that in my obedience to GOD that *Prophetic Guidance* will bless you on your prophetic journey during this special time that we are living in.

Prophets, practice purity, be true to GOD, obey HIM and apply scripture to the decisions that you make. Most importantly, depend on The HOLY SPIRIT to lead and guide you (Psalm 32:8-KJV).

Prophetess Iris L. Jones

I.
The Making of a Prophet

The prophetic gift cannot be purchased. It can only be imparted into a willing vessel by the Spirit of the true and living GOD. Then once that happens, HE entrusts accountable vessels in the earth realm to train up others in the prophetic. Before one is taught or trained as a prophet in the earth realm, he or she must first be called or ordained by GOD. It is more than speaking or declaring and decreeing and the word comes to pass. Being a prophet is a lifestyle. Operating in the prophetic requires a lifestyle change.

Think of it as you being an individual who has a profession in the secular world. He or she is known for their area of expertise. The same idea applies to the life of a prophet. Their specialty requires more than prophesying to people. Therefore, paying for prophetic training does not make one a prophet. A prophet lives a life in alignment with GOD'S desires. What makes a prophet *"true"* is that he or she lives by every word that proceeds out of the mouth of GOD. They may try to do what they want at times, but they will receive rebuke from The LORD. They continue to repeat this cycle until they become submitted to HIS Will. Prophets do not live based on what people do for them, they live by bread alone:

"But Jesus told him, 'No! The Scriptures say, "People do not live by bread alone, but by every word that comes from the mouth of God" Matthew 4:4- NLT.

A prophet should not listen to the inner-me (enemy) of their soul when GOD has given them instructions to follow. They must rebuke the enemy no matter how they feel, as JESUS did in scripture. HE reminded the devil that obeying GOD was more important than succumbing to fleshly hunger. JESUS set the best example for prophets to follow by obeying GOD, communicating with HIM and by remaining humble.

Eli helped young prophet Samuel to effectively hear the voice of GOD. Sometimes GOD will use an imperfect vessel to help a true prophet sharpen their gifts, although no prophet is perfect.

"Then the LORD called Samuel. "Here I am," Samuel responded. He ran to Eli and said, "Here I am. You called me." "I didn't call you," Eli replied. "Go back to bed." So Samuel went back and lay down. The LORD called Samuel again. Samuel got up, went to Eli, and said, "Here I am. You called me." "I didn't call you, son," he responded. "Go back to bed." Samuel had no experience with the LORD, because the LORD's word had not yet been revealed to him. The LORD called Samuel a third time. Samuel got up, went to Eli, and said, "Here I am. You called me." Then Eli realized that the LORD was calling the boy. "Go, lie down," Eli told Samuel. "When he calls you, say, 'Speak, LORD. I'm listening.'" So Samuel went and lay down in his room. The LORD came and stood there. He called as he had called the other times: "Samuel! Samuel!" And Samuel replied, "Speak. I'm listening"-1 Samuel 3:4-10- GW.

Scripture proves that it takes time before one called as a prophet of GOD, knows that they are specifically hearing HIS voice. Samuel was learning how to discern GOD'S voice while under the tutelage of Eli, but Eli did not know that Samuel was hearing GOD until the third time that Samuel came to him. A prophet does not understand that they are called just by having a one-time encounter with a mysterious voice.

Abraham, whose historical and spiritual relationship with GOD preceded Samuel's, relied on the voice of GOD. He was a prophet, called *Father to the faith*. Biblical evidence points to this in

Genesis 20:7, KJV. Abraham was ordained, called and covered by GOD and it is obvious when HE visits Abimelech in a dream:

"Now return the man's wife, for he is a prophet, and he will pray for you and you will live. But if you do not return her, you may be sure that you and all who belong to you will die"- Genesis 20:7, NIV.

GOD protects HIS prophets, "Do not my prophets any harm" (1 Chronicles 16:22, KJV). A sign of the true calling of the prophet is that GOD will harm those who hurt HIS chosen vessels.

Abimelech feared the LORD in that, he obeyed the command to free Abraham and his wife. A prophet in GOD'S eyes, is dear to HIM, someone beyond special; a covenant mouthpiece. A prophet is the one who GOD shares HIS secrets with (Amos 3:7, KJV). Secrets are **not** to be revealed. What is happening is that many prophets or prophetic people want to tell everything that GOD shares. There is a time for revelation but everything that GOD discloses to HIS prophet is **not** to be shared with everyone. There has to be an intimate relationship between GOD and HIS prophet in order for HIM to reveal what is dear to HIS heart. GOD considers HIS prophet, a close friend.

King David developed a close relationship with GOD. He was one who GOD testified about saying "I have found David son of Jesse a man after my own heart; he will do everything I want HIM to do"- Acts 13:22, NIV. JESUS CHRIST is another example of one who did everything that GOD wanted HIM to do. HE fulfilled His assignment on Earth as a true prophet. This is why the spirit of prophecy is the testimony of JESUS CHRIST.

One who is called as a prophet must always acknowledge JESUS CHRIST through his (her) works, confess that JESUS CHRIST is the Son of GOD, and complete their assignment while exalting the Name of JESUS above every name (Philippians 2:9-11, Parallel), or he (she) is not a true prophet of GOD.

A consistent prayer life is one of the mandated prerequisites for one considered a prophet. In fact, prayer is a requirement for any believer to have an intimate, connected relationship with GOD. Think of it this way, any successful relationship requires strong communication. There must be a steady interaction amongst the parties involved so that everyone is aware of his or her role in the relationship. A prophet called by GOD has to communicate with GOD consistently. In fact, most of the dialogue comes from the mouth of GOD and the prophet is to be an active listener.

Prophets must listen carefully to GOD so that they convey the message given to them in a clear, accurate way.

The prophet is not to leave the people confused when he or she delivers a message from The LORD, for GOD is not the author of confusion. When Samuel heard a voice calling him forth, he did not understand that the voice had a distinct sound. Prophets, your responsibility is to know the voice of GOD at all times, and to discern when your ego is speaking.

Apostle Paul says in 1 Corinthians 15:31, NKJV "I die every day!" Prophets, you cannot be vessels of sin! Apostle Paul demonstrates that as he grows in CHRIST JESUS, that his flesh succumbs to sin. Our bodies are temples of the HOLY SPIRIT, and while this is for all of us who are believers, it is especially true for prophets. In order to be effective in the things of the prophetic, you must cast away all known and unknown sin. No fornication, no lustful thoughts, no disrespect to others, and the list goes on and on.

Whatever The LORD tells you to do, obey HIM. Whatever the Word of GOD speaks against, you must speak against it too. No, it is not easy to live holy but, it should not be as difficult when you have a relationship with GOD. Scripture teaches us that "there is nothing too hard for GOD," Jeremiah 32:27, KJV. CHRIST offered up HIS body as a living sacrifice so that we could be healed of any sin that tries to hinder us from being effectively used by GOD. Prophets must stay repentant, in prayer and fast often. Prophets, our flesh must die to any type of sin!

While GOD called many and chose few into the prophetic, remember that just because HE called you, does not mean that you can conduct yourself in a disrespectful manner. We are not to place the blame on GOD and say, "Well GOD, you know me." No! We have to instead humble ourselves, be about our Father's business and affirm that, "GOD, I must fight the good fight of faith, and live to serve you."

In servanthood, we are to crucify the flesh, drop our nets and follow GOD. Before your mother's womb, you accepted the assignment to be a prophet to the nations, after all.

As a prophet called to the nations, you will not be the only one to influence a specific region in our world. GOD has a plethora of assignments for each of HIS prophetic vessels to accomplish. One prophet may be assigned to a regional part of the nations to pray for the sick or feed those suffering from hunger, while another prophet is assigned prophetically to speak to those who rule over certain governments.

He or she may not travel to another country. As prophetic ministers, do not burden yourselves with thinking that, you are only assigned to a specific area, region or part of the world. The prophetic covers a multitude of cultures and populations and does not discriminate in serving others. As one flows in the things of GOD they are speaking as GOD says to speak, and decreeing what HE says to decree. GOD is Omnipresent and the prophetic word is not restrained by whether one is traveling the world or not.

II.
The Bible is Prophecy

The books in the Bible are a prophecy of what has occurred in the past, what is taking place now and what will happen in the future:

"In the beginning was the Word, and the Word was with GOD, and the Word was GOD" John 1:1- KJV.

This scripture is key in prophesying to all believers because it expresses to the us that the Word of GOD is just as important as the other two members of the Trinity (Son & Holy Spirit). Whenever we are dealing with a trial, the Word tells us that we have the victory and we eventually win.

The Word teaches us how to deal with situations, and how to pray. Even in this day and age there is not one dilemma that arises that the Bible does not foretell us of, or provides a solution for. GOD has always kept us in mind. Before many people knew that they would be sick, a prophecy in the Bible was provided to tell them that they were healed.

While so much is happening in the world and things seem to be out of control, the LORD tells us through HIS Word to humble ourselves, pray and turn from our wicked ways (2 Chronicles 7:14).

GOD provides a solution before we realize that there is a problem. Prophecies about how to deal with our lives were recorded before our very existence. That is powerful! The Bible provides us with a variety of prophetic individuals to learn from. No prophet is the same. Regardless of our function in the Body of CHRIST, GOD made us all unique. We are a part of one body, but have different missions. We are to cooperate with one another and bring forth the Word of the LORD that will save HIS people. Prophets are unique and unlike any other prophet.

The Bible is a compilation of passages that illustrate communication between GOD and man. The men or women that HE gave specific assignments to are the prophets. They foretell of things to come, and convey these messages to people. GOD is Omnipotent and knows everything, including our future:

"And do not forget the many times I clearly told you what was going to happen in the future. For I am God- I only- and there is no other like me who can tell you what is going to happen. All I say will come to pass, for I do whatever I wish" Isaiah 46:9-10- TLB.

Prophecy is systematically aligned to scripture. Individuals who effectively prophesy are filled with the Word and the pneumatikos of GOD. They understand that "Man does not live by bread alone..." and that GOD is the Chief Prophet, speaking through the human prophet in the earth realm. These prophecies in the Bible told us of a Savior who would come and die for our sins (Luke 24:46-47, NKJV). No prophecy from GOD was produced by the will of man, but only by the Will of GOD:

"And we have something more sure, the prophetic word, to which you will do well to pay attention as to a lamp shining in a dark place, until the day dawns and the morning star rises in your hearts, knowing this first of all, that no prophecy of Scripture comes from someone's own interpretation. For no prophecy was ever produced by the will of man, but men spoke from God as they were carried along by the Holy Spirit" 2 Peter 1:19-21-ESV.

No prophecy spoken through a prophet from GOD, speaks against HIS Word or tries to change GOD'S intention for HIS believers. Remember, the Word was GOD (John 1:1, NLT). Therefore, there can be no separation from GOD as a prophet.

When the word of the LORD goes forth, it must be confirmed by GOD first, and then it will eventually witness to the recipient of the word. No word spoken by a prophet of GOD should speak against HIS law, commands or HIS promises. The Word is to edify, exhort, and comfort the hearer of it (1 Corinthians 14:3-KJV).

While some prophecies released by true prophets have yet to come to pass, they shall. Biblical prophecy is GOD'S way of communicating to HIS people of what is to come. We must examine the validity of prophecy and not crucify the prophetic, but depend on The HOLY SPIRIT for prophetic instruction and guidance on how to release what GOD is saying (2 Peter 1:20-21-ESV). The Bible teaches all who read it and correctly interpret it, sound doctrine and the correct parameters in which prophecy should be released, received and stewarded over.

III.
Dimensions of the Prophetic

There are dimensions of the prophetic that determine the *temporary* or *permanent* existence of prophetic gifting. All of the dimensions are not entirely discussed in this book, but readers will have a general idea of the types that exist, and the purpose for them on Earth.

The office of the prophet

Apostle Paul operated in the office of a prophet and a teacher before being appointed to the ministry of an apostle (Acts 13:1, KJV). One in the prophetic office speaks with governmental authority. This authority is uttered from the heavens as the prophet represents GOD'S government. When the prophet receives their mantle from GOD, they are able to flow in this realm.

GOD appointed HIS prophets to be 2nd in rank in HIS government:

"And GOD hath set some in the church, first apostles, secondarily prophets, thirdly teachers, after that miracles, then gifts of healings, helps, governments, diversity of tongues" 1 Corinthians 12:28- KJV.

Prophets along with the Apostles who are 1st in rank in GOD'S government are the foundation of the church:

"What a foundation you stand on now: the apostles and the prophets; and the cornerstone of the building is Jesus Christ himself!" Ephesians 2:20- TLB.

JESUS is the establisher of the office of the prophet and is the highest ranking general. That is why it is absolutely important for a prophet to lead people to HIM, whose life came about as a result of a prophecy from an angel:

"And the angel came in unto her, and said, "Hail, thou that art highly favored, the Lord is with thee: blessed art thou among women. And when she saw him, she was troubled at his saying, and cast in her mind what manner of salutation this should be. And the angel said unto her, Fear not, Mary, for thou hast found favor with GOD. And, behold, thou shalt conceive in thy womb, and bring forth a son, and shalt call his name Jesus. He shall be great, and shall be called the Son of the Highest: and the Lord GOD shall give unto him the throne of his father David" Luke 1:28-32- KJV.

A supernatural seed can only bring forth a highly trusted, supernatural spokesman who was made manifest in the flesh, for the Kingdom of GOD. As the Son of GOD, JESUS would be the representative for what is to come because of HIS direct communication with Heaven. Those of us that are truly called to the office of the prophet, only declare what the Heavens communicate to us by way of the greatest intercessor, JESUS. "On earth as it is in heaven…" Matthew 6:10-KJV.

What John the Baptist says about JESUS in John 3 explains HIS office as a Chief Prophet of the Kingdom of GOD:

"John replied, "God in heaven appoints each man's work. My work is to prepare the way for that man so that everyone will go to him. You yourselves know how plainly I told you that I am not the Messiah. I am here to prepare the way for him—that is all. The crowds will naturally go to the main attraction— the bride will go where the bridegroom is! A bridegroom's friends rejoice with him. I am the Bridegroom's friend, and I am filled with joy at his success. He must become greater and greater, and I must become less and less" John 3:27-30-MSG.

The one called to the office of the prophet speaks things into being with a heavenly backing that results in signs following.

This is why prophets must be careful of what they say. Those who hold a position in this governmental office cannot speak anything other than what GOD says, no matter how they feel. They are not differentiated by their gender (*i.e. prophet for male, prophetess for female*). A prophet is more than a gender; they operate in a spiritual gift that brings about supernatural happenings.

As the bridegroom, JESUS is the foundation of all prophets, regardless of their function in the Body of CHRIST. HE s the Chief Cornerstone. It is absolutely important to understand, that while HE also holds offices as the only sinless Son of GOD, The High Priest, Master Teacher, and our Lord and Savior, HE is also the leading governmental official over all prophets. It is through HIM that the true prophets release the word of GOD, with mirac es, and manifestations following. Prophets are a gift from JESUS CHRIST to HIS Bride, the church.

If one is called by GOD into the prophetic office, he or she must keep his or her ear to HIS mouth at all times. They are not to utter a word that precedes any move of GOD. They are to be very sensitive to the move of GOD and fear HIM. GOD reveals what is important to HIS prophets; they are entrusted vessels who are not to reveal all of the information that they receive from HIM.

Those operating in the prophetic office are to be unapologetically bold when delivering HIS word, but more importantly he or she must be obedient to GOD. Heaven has a sound that many will not be able to recognize or comprehend. As a representative of the Bridegroom, every prophet's responsibility is to prepare HIS Bride for HIS arrival.

When one operates in an office, they are not functioning in a gift. The office of the prophet has the authority to function in a higher rank than the gift of prophecy. Those called to the prophetic office have the same right to prophesy and preach to a congregation as a pastor who preaches to their congregation and provides pastoral counseling.

In no way is a prophet to overstep the position of a pastor's authority in a local church. However, many called to the prophetic office also pastor. As one of the fivefold ministry gifts, the prophet is responsible for serving in his or her call to the Body of CHRIST. That includes providing guidance, correction, instruction, rebuke and revelation. Those called to the office of the prophet function in all of the ministries of the Old Testament prophets, and represent the New Testament prophet, JESUS CHRIST. Whatever JESUS speaks for the purifying of HIS Church, is spoken through the one called to the prophetic office.

The prophetic intercessor

Prophetic intercessors pray and war in the spirit realm against the powers of darkness that fight against the Kingdom of GOD. Dark does not like light, and the enemy would like for the world to remain blind to the power of GOD. For GOD to show anyone what is to come before it happens, an example shows us the need for intercessors:

"And I sought for a man among them who shall build up a wall that I should not destroy it but I found none," Ezekiel 22:30- NKJV.

GOD trusts you to pray regarding what is to come. Often, an intercessor causes GOD to change HIS mind or the least, to have mercy on those that

HE would not. Many will refute that GOD does not change HIS mind but indeed he does. HE does not change HIS mind like humans do.

HIS *mind change* is that HE grieves the outcome of those who disobey HIM. HE grieved about the actions of King Saul, who after a long history of disobedience and false repentance superseded him obeying GOD, as well as his obedience to prophet Samuel. GOD relented in Exodus chapter 32 when HE did not bring the disaster on the people as HE said that he would.

What the Bible demonstrates to readers is that, GOD is not a man to lie (Numbers 23), but through HIS grace and mercy HE does consider the hearts of those who truly repent. True intercessors have that type of heart. They repent and plead with GOD to have mercy.

GOD showed compassion to the people of Nineveh when they truthfully repented (Jonah 3:4-9). It took the prayers and intercession of Jonah for GOD'S grace to be shown. A prophetic intercessor can also have a temporary assignment. What this means is that they may not be used to intercede or help someone for a season. Some intercessors are only visible to the individual that they are assigned to help for one specific event.

The evangelist Philip was used as a prophetic intercessor to show up as the Ethiopian eunuch began to seek more about his life and his purpose in ministry.

"And the Spirit said to Philip, "Go over and join this chariot." So Philip ran to him and heard him reading Isaiah the prophet and asked, "Do you understand what you are reading?" And he said, "How can I, unless someone guides me?" And he invited Philip to come up and sit with him" Acts 8:29-31-ESV.

Here, is an example of Philip being prophetically led by the voice of GOD to travel to a specific location in order to guide an individual to JESUS CHRIST.

Again, the "Testimony of JESUS is the spirit of prophecy." If JESUS is not the center of the testimony, then the spirit of prophecy is null and void. In this example the prophetic was used at a specific time, for a specific purpose which resulted in a man being transformed into a vessel for GOD to use to minister to others, the Good News of JESUS CHRIST.

The prophetic voice of the Church

Unlike other books that discuss the dimensions of the prophetic, we should consider the voice of the church. It seems as though there is a movement of people prophesying in the church, without the church moving in and embracing the prophetic.

Is the gift of the prophetic being handled correctly in the church? Is a word from The LORD being released to build the church, or is there a separation of the church from the prophetic? These are all questions that the HOLY SPIRIT wants us to ponder. Revelation 2:29, KJV tells us "He that hath an ear, let him hear what the Spirit saith to the churches."

In the scripture preceding the final verse of chapter 2, JESUS shares how necessary it is for the church to be pure and holy. Here, there is no reference solely to the four walls as we often associate with the word *church*, but instead to the **Church** which CHRIST calls HIS bride. All of us, who dedicate our lives to JESUS and the testimony of HIS life that gives us true salvation, should understand the elements of the church, in which HE is referencing. The prophetic voice is a continuous reminder to assess our fruits as members of the Body of CHRIST. Also in the book of Revelation, CHRIST warns us of what we should and should not do as a church. We should seek HIM, and depend on HIM. We should not fall for the works of the false prophet, or prophetic:

"Whoever has ears, let them hear what the Spirit says to the churches. To the one who is victorious, I will give some of the hidden manna. I will also give that person a white stone with a new name written on it, known only to the one who receives it" Revelation 2:17-NIV.

An important point is made here. CHRIST'S reference to *"hidden manna"* is a reminder that when the covenant was made in the Old Testament, that Moses instructed Aaron to put two quarts of manna flakes in a jar which was placed in the ark of the covenant for future generations to see (see Exodus 16:31-33, KJV). The church has forgotten these heavenly instructions. They view this manna as a keepsake instead of the bread of the living GOD that will feed us and keep us through any famine or destruction in the earth realm or any threat to the covenant that we have with our GOD. The church has instead fallen for what JESUS

CHRIST warns us about in Revelation 2:20-23 (KJV):

"Nevertheless, I have this against you: You tolerate that woman Jezebel, who calls herself a prophet. By her teaching she misleads my servants into sexual immorality and the eating of food sacrificed to idols. I have given her time to repent of her immorality, but she is unwilling. So I will cast her on a bed of suffering, and I will make those who commit adultery with her suffer intensely, unless they repent of her ways. I will strike her children dead. Then all the churches will know that I am he who searches hearts and minds, and I will repay each of you according to your deeds."

Manna meaning *"What is it?"* in Hebrew (man hu') was created by GOD to demonstrate to us as believers that something as supernatural as white coriander seeds could supply our needs because GOD intentionally desires to take care of us. Whether we believe that manna is our supply is dependent on our personal belief system of who GOD is in our life. Do we believe HIM to be all powerful and to be our supply in this same manner? Or, do we read the Old Testament and comprehend it as "another narrative" without believing the entire word of the living GOD?

What seems to have happened is that the church has allowed the false teachers to come in and depreciate the voice that is the designated messenger of all true churches, the voice of our LORD and SAVIOR JESUS CHRIST. As a result, distraction, attacks, burdens and disbelief began to overtake the Body of CHRIST. It is very easy for the adversary to creep in with teachings as JESUS refers to as "Satan's so-called deep secrets" (Revelation 2:24, KJV). When the church receives such false teachings, burdens result. JESUS continues to say "I will not impose any other burden on you, except to hold on to what you have (the truth) until I come"- Revelation 2:24, KJV).

As the true church of GOD, we must be accountable and refrain from blaming the adversary for all that happens in our spiritual and natural lives. We should examine the *body* and find the area that the spirit of deception has crept into, then cleanse the body with the Blood of JESUS and align ourselves with the Word. The Body of CHRIST must die daily to the world's influence so that we do not mirror anything but the earthly version of the Kingdom of GOD and its righteousness.

The gift of prophecy

It was mentioned earlier in this chapter that the prophetic intercessor can operate under a temporary anointing. When concerning the prophetic gifts similarities can arise. Many people have a problem with this and believe that "once a prophet, always a prophet." Some even believe this idea concerning each of the ministry gifts or seven gifts of the Spirit mentioned in 1 Corinthians 12:4-6 (NIRV):

"There are different kinds of gifts. But they are all given to believers by the same Spirit. There are different ways to serve. But all gifts come from the same GOD. There are diverse ways that the Spirit moves. But the same God is working in all these ways and in all people."

To think that you or anyone else cannot be used prophetically for a time or season is not sensible. As prophets, be grateful when GOD uses you but be humble when HE uses others. There are many people that are operating out of their season, who refuse to humble themselves, and yield to the new plan that GOD has for their life. For example, there are an influx of prophets who become apostles, but is this GOD'S true intention for them? Who were you before you knew that you were a prophet? Were you an usher or a lay member attending church services weekly?

There are many in the professional work setting that seek additional education and training. They are not necessarily promoted to a new position because of this. Sometimes a promotion occurs but not all of the time, because of the additional education and training that has been acquired. Even when we are trained in ministry, we are to be wise enough to discern if we are self-promoting ourselves, or if GOD is truly promoting us.

The gift of prophecy is circumstantial and a revelation from GOD for a particular moment. The benefit at this level of gifting is that it speaks to a situation in the present. It does not speak of the past or future. An example is when the Holy Spirit spoke directly to the Church at Antioch. The prophets who were used are described as those "Who spoke a *new* message of GOD to the people..." Acts 13:1-2-Amplified.

The gift of prophecy is not to be disregarded if the gift is temporarily activated. The ability to hear the voice of GOD is a true gift and HE can revisit the individuals that HE used to share that word at another time. For those used in this realm of prophecy, it does not mean that your gift is not appreciated by others or that GOD does not love you. It takes a mature and willing vessel to understand that any spiritual gift assigned from the Ruach of GOD must complete and fulfill their assignment. There are many parts to the body, just as in prophecy, there are many pieces to put together in GOD'S prophetic puzzle.

Word of knowledge and word of wisdom

What is misunderstood by many is that both the word of knowledge and the word of wisdom are prophetic spiritual gifts given to benefit and bless the Church as a whole. What must be included when teaching on the prophetic is that revelatory gifts are very prophetic and are released through a vessel by the Ruach of GOD.

1 Corinthians 12:7 (TLB) shows us what every believer under submission to the HOLY SPIRIT has the ability to do: "The Holy Spirit displays God's power through each of us as a means of helping the entire church."

If the word of knowledge and the word of wisdom are not prophetic or revelatory then why are they highlighted in scripture as Spiritual gifts that edify the Body of CHRIST?

"He gives power for doing miracles to some, and to others power to prophesy and preach. He gives someone else the power to know whether evil spirits are speaking through those who claim to be giving God's messages-- or whether it is really the Spirit of God who is speaking" 1 Corinthians 12:10-TLB.

What mature believers of GOD and HIS Son JESUS CHRIST must do is castrate the plans of the enemy to muzzle and destroy the prophetic voices on Earth. Through much observation of what is occurring in churches all over the world, it appears that rank in title in the Earth realm has somehow superseded the Spiritual gifts that are described in scripture.

Operating in some form of spiritual gifts is expected of every believer of GOD, however we must be sure that our gifts are not demonstrative of confusion and surely come from GOD (1 Corinthians 14:33-KJV).

IV.
The Prophetic Mantle

To possess a mantle means that you have something valuable. It is not something that detaches from you because your body is occupied with the mantle that you have possession of. Unlike operating in the anointing for a short time frame, to carry a mantle is to maintain something permanently.

To further clarify, a person who is anointed to prophesy does not make them a prophet, or a person anointed to preach does not qualify him or her to pastor. King Saul prophesied while in the company of others, but unlike Elijah, he was not called to a prophetic office or position. The *office* on Elijah's life is evident because when the mantle on his life fell upon Elisha, the company of prophets said "The spirit of Elijah is resting on Elisha!" 2 Kings 2:15-Amplified. We must recognize that having an anointing does not necessarily mean that one contains a spiritual mantle from GOD.

Once it is identified that there is a difference between having an *anointing* and holding a *mantle*, the Kingdom of GOD will advance. The kingdom of darkness will not be able to overrule the flesh of those who are operating in incorrect positions, offices, and anointings. King Saul teaches a valuable lesson about operating outside of the will of GOD. He rivaled against David because he wanted everything that David had. David was mantled the future king while King Saul ruled Israel as an anointed king.

The difference is that while David was publicly anointed with a flask of oil, GOD assigned a willing prophet to publicly affirm and cover David with HIS Spirit and mantle. King David is described as a man who the Spirit of GOD dwelled upon at *all* times, becoming the source of his wisdom, intelligence and prophetic abilities. King Saul did not possess these qualities and that is why he grew reliant on the approval of man until he lost the complete favor of GOD. Saul's anointing was temporary while David's operation in the anointing of GOD was backed by a mantle of authority, prominence and kingship.

The prophetic mantle cannot be taught by experts or bought. Elisha had to leave his place of wealth and prestige to catch the anointing of another prophet. If you want a prophetic mantle it will not be transferred to you in any other way. This can be very difficult to understand especially when you are anointed. You may feel that it does not take following others in order to behold a mantle, but it does. Elisha's intention was not to gain a mantle, but to become close to Elijah because he saw GOD working through him and knew that the works were authentic, and only glorified The LORD.

When you carry a prophetic mantle you will not be perfect. However, I warn every believer-- **please do not make being "imperfect" an excuse to do whatever you feel like doing, even though you may have character flaws.** Elijah had some issues with his character. While he was very bold in sharing the word of The LORD, the spirit of fear ran him around town and into hiding places.

Imagine being mentored by someone who pressures you to be strong in the sight of The Lord, yet they feel like giving up. A mantle is to be passed to the one being mentored. It is wise to remain faithful even when you want to part ways. That is, if the person that you are being mentored by is assigned to transfer a mantle to you.

When you have a prophetic mantle, some people are not to be mentored by you. If the individuals that seek you out are not humble or teachable they are not genuinely your assignment and their fruit will prove that they are not. A student or mentee should not challenge your prophetic authority. When the spiritual potency of your mantle impacts them they will seek you out:

"Elijah went to Elisha and put his coat on Elisha. Elisha immediately left his oxen and ran after Elijah. Elisha said, "Let me kiss my mother and father goodbye. Then I will follow you." Elijah answered, "You can do that. I will not stop you."

Elisha turned away from him and went back. He killed the oxen and used the yoke for firewood. He boiled the meat, gave it to the people, and they all ate together. Then Elisha went to follow Elijah and became his helper" 1 Kings 19:19-21-ERV.

When one has an authentic prophetic mantle from GOD there is evidence to prove it. The most convincing evidence is that one is 1) humble, and 2) teachable. Elisha was humble in that he endured Elijah's tough mentorship because he was teachable. He knew that Elijah had a very close relationship with GOD and that he would not mislead him. Elisha was teachable even when Elijah compared himself to others, suffered depression, and when he did not want Elisha to witness his transition. One thing you must ask yourself as a mentee is, "Am I willing to follow the one who has my mantle regardless of their character flaws?"

Too many people have disconnected from others before the assignment was complete and this is why there is a spirit of agitation, aggravation and manipulation that has overwhelmed many in the Body of CHRIST. If you know that you should be mentored and that there is a prophetic mantle waiting to be transferred to you, repent, pray and believe that GOD will lead you to the right mentor. It will happen especially if GOD has an assignment for you to release prophetic mantles to others while you are on this earth.

V.
The Journey of a Prophet

Prophets grapple with and experience spiritual and natural journeys often. They relocate regularly and are seldom comfortable in one place for a long period of time, especially when they are running from GOD. A great deal of the prophetic ministry is wrestling with GOD. Like Elijah, we try to tell GOD that there are no true prophets like us and that no one will receive our message. We do our best to convince HIM into believing that we cannot handle the task. Then the wrestling begins as well as the chastening.

"So Jacob was left alone, and a man wrestled with him till daybreak…" Genesis 32:24- NIV.

Jacob is an example of how GOD will take you through seasons of distress only to bless you because you eventually trust HIM. He needed a place of refuge and sought much consolation from The LORD. He was told to return to his homeland where his angered brother Esau awaited his arrival. With the fear that he embodied, he obeyed because GOD told him that HE would protect him.

For Jacob, his return to his homeland was also a spiritual journey because he returned to the place where GOD promised to bless him. As a prophet, your assigned journey on the way to your destination may not be easy, but obedience is the key to doors opening for you. GOD changed Jacob's name when he responded to his fear with obedience. He learned how to hold on to GOD'S unchanging hand even through the difficult times of the journey. An indication that you are on an assigned prophetic journey is that no matter what circumstances you face, GOD will send angels to comfort, protect and guide you:

"As Jacob started on his way again, angels of GOD came to meet him. When Jacob saw them, he exclaimed, "This is GOD'S camp!"-Genesis 32:1-2 NLT.

GOD will send an angel to help you to fight against your flesh that tries to convince you that you cannot fulfill the call on your life or that no one will accept you. When this "man" wrestled with Jacob, it was in the darkness of the night, descriptive of Jacob's life. He is filled with fear, despair, and gloom. When he initially begins to fight, he did not know who he wrestled with. When crippled by the angel of The LORD, he surrendered his will to fight to the assailant in the dark. When daybreak arrives, he realizes who this person is and decides that he will hold on so that he can be blessed.

Prophets of GOD must grasp the fact that they are assigned to fulfill the Will of GOD regarding the testimony of JESUS CHRIST. Your journey will consist of character assassination, name calling, verbal disqualification of your ministry gift or mantle, insecurity, depression, worry, anxiety and the desire to no longer be a prophet. These emotions arise and situations like this happen when GOD is shifting you from *"Jacob" to "Israel."*

You must confess who you are to GOD before HE can truly use you and bless you. Are you a liar, a thief, a manipulator, insecure, jealous, envious and wonder why GOD wants to use you? The referenced scriptures in this book are a good place to begin as you examine the imperfections that many humans have. GOD continues to show us that HE will not allow those who HE has called to fail when our obedience pleases HIM.

Another biblical example of the repercussions of choosing not to fully obey the prophetic journey that GOD has created for your life is found in 1 Kings 13. First, when GOD gives us an assignment we should not disclose all of the details. Amos 3:7 tells us that GOD reveals HIS secrets to HIS servant, the prophet. Some people may not agree with this statement but there is no need to tell all of your GOD given instructions to others when HE sends you to complete an assignment.

"But the man of God said to the king, "Even if you were to give me half your house (wealth), I would not go with you, nor would I eat bread or drink water in this place. For I was commanded by the word of the Lord, 'You shall not eat bread or drink water, nor shall you return by the way you came'"-1 Kings 13:8-9, KJV.

Unfortunately, many should not know your journey or the specifics of your assignment because distraction often presents itself. Having experienced a similar situation, it is quite easy to share information with others because we want to prove that we are regular human beings. But, prophets are set apart. At times we overly explain ourselves because we do not want others to misunderstand us.

Some people will accuse you of abandoning them as you work for the Kingdom of GOD but when you have a GOD ordained assignment, you have to choose who you will serve. Some people will be upset with you because they do not understand why GOD called you. Some will be angry with you because you are obedient to the call and will pretend to support you. This is a type of distraction as well. Another major interference that often attacks the ministry and spiritual gifts in the Body of CHRIST is the spirit of *familiarity*.

The spirit of familiarity will have one comparing themselves to others, if they are not aware of the warning signs. This happens with the obedient prophet in 1 Kings 13. When word about the healing that he performed on the king circulates around Bethel, he encounters a disobedient prophet:

"He answered him, "I too am a prophet, as you are; and an angel spoke to me by the word of the LORD, saying, 'Bring him back with you to your house, so that he may eat bread and drink water.'" *But* he lied to him. So the man of God went back with him, and ate bread in his house and drank water" -1 Kings 13:18-19-Amplified.

A person that has a familiar spirit will compare their life to yours, their experiences to yours, their spirituality to yours, and will even compare their relationship with GOD to yours. This is why it is imperative that you obey the commands of The LORD because people will deceive you and many times they do not even know why they are doing it.

It is a spirit within them that is grounded in disobedience. A disobedient spirit emerges from a spirit of disbelief. When a parent tells their child to complete chores or they will be grounded and the child does not obey, he or she is operating in a form of disbelief. They do not believe that they will get grounded, or they do not care about the consequences that are connected to not completing the chores.

So is the case with the disobedient prophet who is noted in scripture as "old." While this prophet is older in age, he is called old because his disobedience disqualified the anointing on his life. This can happen. The anointing that was upon Saul left his life, and he also was replaced (1 Samuel 16:14, KJV). Operating in familiarity results in complications that can affect your prophetic destiny:

"And as they sat at the table, the word of the Lord came to the prophet who had brought him back. And he cried to the man of God who came from Judah, "Thus says the Lord, 'Because you have disobeyed the word of the Lord and have not kept the command that the Lord your God commanded you, but have come back and have eaten bread and drunk water in the place of which he said to you, "Eat no bread and drink no water," your body shall not come to the tomb of your fathers.'" And after he had eaten bread and drunk, he saddled the donkey for the prophet whom he had brought back. And as he went away a lion met him on the road and killed him" 1 Kings 13:20-24, KJV.

Disobedience to GOD is an obvious offense to HIM. If there is anything that the old prophet learned when the younger prophet was killed for stopping while on his prophetic journey to have dinner with him, is that GOD judges our disobedience, especially when we are expected to complete the assignment that is given to us.

VI.
Prophetic Integrity

What does it mean to be integral? As a prophet, your mindset, your actions, your lifestyle, and your journey must be reflective of reverential behaviors. You must represent the Kingdom of GOD cheerfully and decently with order. Often, there are individuals who have a great anointing and operate remarkably in their area of spiritual gifting, but their character exceeds a flaw or some flaws, even. A great deal of their attitude is disrespectful to Kingdom principles, which is disregarding of who GOD is as well as the assignment that HE has given us.

You will have to learn how to crucify your own flesh, fight many adversarial attacks and while things may not go the way you would like them to, you are expected to walk in agape love. Your life becomes a disciple to CHRIST. The way that you talk, minister, treat your family and loved ones, your colleagues, and those who have betrayed you determines a level of maturity and just how integral you are.

Truthfully, there will be many people who will still deem you unaccountable, irrational, fruitless and incompetent to be used in the capacity that GOD is using you. Yet, the test of integrity that you will have to endure is inclusive of walking in the love of GOD, because of your love for HIM. The *love* walk is not easy. Apostle Paul teaches us this when he is on his prophetic assignment to transform the Jews into believers of JESUS CHRIST. As a former persecutor of believers, he learned what it felt like to be crucified by other people when he was transformed by the saving grace of GOD:

"We are often troubled, but not crushed; sometimes in doubt, but never in despair; there are many enemies, but we are never without a friend; and though badly hurt at times, we are not destroyed. At all times we carry in our mortal bodies the death of Jesus, so that his life also may be seen in our bodies" -2 Corinthians 4:8-10, KJV.

Your character will be tested often, especially by your enemies. But what about when those who you love test you too? There are some individuals that may have been mentored by you who will test your love walk. They will question your authority, magnify your mistakes and they may disclose your flaws to others.

Your life and what you stand for will be tested, often. Anyone called to the five-fold ministry will have to learn this but prophets, must learn and practice how to shake the dust off of their feet on a regular basis. This is the only way that you will be distraction free from the thoughts of people. It is a spirit of familiarity that you must leave behind and "press toward the mark of the high calling in CHRIST JESUS" -Philippians 3:14, NIV.

You have to forget what you have been through. If you hold on to the past it will affect your present and your future. It is not easy to forget things, but when GOD transforms your mind, HE will remove certain things from your memory. Think of it this way:

You are a computer and your database has been wiped clean. There is no history of your past rights or wrongs, or a record of what has been done to you. We must remember that when we are new creatures in CHRIST that old things have passed away.

One way to determine if someone walks in integrity is that they will not allow past situations to navigate their present reality. If we say that we are called by GOD, we must demonstrate it in our actions or HIS spirit is not effective in our lives:

"All of us, then, who are mature should take such a view of things. And if on some point you think differently, that too God will make clear to you. Only let us live up to what we have already attained"- Philippians 3:15-NIV.

Integral prophets with Godly character reflect a lifestyle and behavior of maturity that is grounded in the most excellent gift.

"But above all, you should want the more important gifts. But now I will show you the best way of all"-1 Corinthians 12:31.

Love should be our most important focus as the Good News of JESUS CHRIST is shared with the multitudes. This is the reason that anyone should be involved in ministry. In order to survive in the Kingdom of GOD as an effective messenger you must be obedient to GOD, live a life of consistent repentance and walk in agape love. It is the only way that your ministry will endure.

Even though GOD called you, you must be sure that you are in ministry for the right reasons. All of us have sinned (turned from following GOD'S strictest directions) and have fallen short of the glory of GOD (Romans 3:23, KJV). However, when one becomes mature in the things of GOD they put away childish mindsets and actions.

Apostle Paul teaches in Ephesians 4:15 to "Speak the truth in love, growing in every way more and more like Christ, who is the head of HIS body, the church." It is recommended that prophets use

Ephesians 4 as a reflective study guide to help them to reflect as they serve in ministry. He or she must remember that every person has a story to tell and wounds to back those stories up, but our outward bleeding will not help the wounded individuals who do not have a relationship with GOD.

As you develop integrally, some areas to pray for more strength and obedience in are:

   1) To be loving and supportive at all times rather than accusing others of their behavior towards you.

   2) For GOD'S help when dealing with the personal highs and lows that occur in ministry.

   3) To fulfill ministry responsibilities confidentially.

   4) To live a godly lifestyle that is reflective of holiness.

   5) To have competent knowledge of the Bible, and an active, consistent prayer life.

You must understand that obeying GOD is far greater than the sacrifices that you make while serving HIM. Your love walk must line up with the greatest commandment that JESUS spoke of.

When it does you will be established on an integral, prophetic journey because your focus is on pleasing GOD.

"Jesus replied: Love the Lord your God with all your heart and with all your soul and with all your mind"- Matthew 22:37-NIV.

As a prophet your character will be tested at every level of your elevation in GOD.

Each level of your prophetic journey can be compared to you being stopped at a checkpoint by a police officer. As a police officer checks your credentials for validity, so do those in the earth and spirit realms:

"Therefore, since we have been justified by faith, we have peace with God through our Lord Jesus Christ. Through him we have also obtained access by faith into this grace in which we stand, and we rejoice in hope of the glory of God. Not only that, but we rejoice in our sufferings, knowing that suffering produces endurance, and endurance produces character, and character produces hope." Romans 5:1-4 ESV.

Prophets are human beings too, but as we mature in GOD, our complaints about what we encounter in our spiritual and natural walk should cease. We should find joy in The LORD for HE is our strength and our strong tower. It is by HIS grace that we are able to stand against the wiles of the enemy. We should not allow bitterness to saturate our souls because we will not be effective for HIS use.

We will fall from HIS glory when we allow another source to consume us. We must stop with the "I am only human" excuse and walk in our prophetic decrees that we are GOD'S mouthpiece and that no one except GOD can touch us or do us any harm. Prophets, remain integral by fasting, praying, repenting and being obedient to GOD or the enemy will creep in and sift you of your godly inheritance.

VII.
Who Needs the Prophet and Who the Prophet Needs

The prophet is not exempt from needing the support of others, spiritual training or tutelage. Prophets need other prophetic people to help them to develop in ministry; this is only after the influence from and close knit relationship with the Ruach of GOD. Scripture teaches us in Amos 3:7 that "Surely the LORD GOD does nothing without revealing HIS secrets to HIS servants the prophets." Prophets must first depend on GOD because that is when HE uses him or her to edify HIS Church.

Every prophet needs someone who will help him or her to align their life with the will of GOD. Actually, no one is excused from having someone to help them to identify the areas of weakness in their life. Nathan is an example of a court prophet who challenged David to align himself with the covenant of GOD: "But that same night the LORD spoke his word to Nathan: "Say to my servant David, 'This is what the LORD says: Are you the one who will build me a house to live in?"- 2 Samuel 7:4-5-GW.

Another example of GOD'S provision of prophetic assistance to a prophet is when David is warned about committing adultery, as well as when he is on his deathbed and Nathan informs him about Adonijah's plot to become king (1 Kings 1, KJV). It was by the intercession of a prophet sent by GOD, that Solomon was able to become king when his father transitioned. Prophets usually do not need many eyes to see for them, but GOD will place a trusted individual in place at the right time so that HIS prophet does not embarrass the Kingdom of GOD. It is the prophet's choice to accept godly wisdom or deny it, which in turn determines their success or failure as a vessel of GOD.

One thing that every believer must be aware of is that while all have sinned and have fallen short of the glory of GOD, that HE takes record of every decision that we make. We are not exempt from HIS chastening, HIS punishment or HIS rebuke. There are many with the prophetic gift who do not believe that they are to remain students of the gospel and teachings of JESUS CHRIST. Scripture tells us that a "student is not greater than his teacher" (Matthew 10:24, NIV).

We as prophets or any member of the five-fold ministry, should behold this truth spoken by JESUS. We are not greater than the Spirit of GOD that leads us, guides us, and teaches us. In order to be successful in ministry and in our personal lives, we must apply biblical teachings to our prophetic and personal demonstrations of faith.

Prophets endure a great deal when they release a message from GOD because when HE speaks, it is from a place of love, and also a place of sharpening. Rebuke is often a form of disregard that man has practiced, while GOD operates in equipping us through the sharpening of HIS Word. When prophets are connected to those through leadership, covering or mentorship they are often misunderstood especially if he or she is completely obedient to the Word of The LORD.

Many that are in leadership positions do not receive counsel from others because they may believe that the individual does not have more authority, credentials or experience than they do. Prophets are an exception to this rule and many may not like that. The prophet's assignment is distinctive. They cannot be boxed in even while they are being developed.

A great deal of their development is through trial and error and chastening from GOD. It takes sold out, humble, obedient and spirit led individuals to walk with a true prophet. Majority of the time, they walk alone but a true vessel of the Ruach of GOD will yield to what GOD is doing through that prophetic individual and remain consistently true to that connection as well as prayerful.

Important enough, a true prophet needs a close knit, non-religious relationship with GOD. In fact, one must be holy for GOD is holy (1 Peter 1:15-17, KJV). That is the only way that we can commune with HIM, grow in HIM and work for HIM with the goal of bringing souls to HIS Kingdom. Prophets must have a strong prayer life. Most of their dialogue is with GOD through extensive prayer time.

It can be difficult to be a prophet as well as a socialite. It is GOD'S desire for you to live a balanced life even when 80% of your life is sold out to HIM. However, living a life of balance does not look like everyone else's life. GOD will bless you with prosperity because you have suffered for HIM, but your prosperity may not look like the next person's prosperity. So never judge what your favor looks like when compared to another.

Never compare what your needs are as a prophet, to others. Your spiritual needs differ depending on the guidance that you have received from both GOD and man. There are some who will not understand your spiritual development and will incriminate your ministry and suggest that you have not been through a process of development to be called a prophet.

You have to know who GOD created you to be, what HE has instructed you to do and pray without ceasing for direction (1 Thessalonians 5:17, NKJV).

You have to be developed by the fruits of the Spirit in order to overcome the disregard, disrespect and immaturity of others. You cannot become like them and hurt others for it is not pleasing to GOD to do so. You must remember that in order to be successful in your prophetic ministry as a prophet to GOD first, that you must be yielded to HIM through HIS Son and obey the leading and guiding of The HOLY SPIRIT.

Prophet, while you do need others because we all need people in order to help GOD to build HIS Kingdom, you must obey GOD and HIS Word first and foremost. This is what is going to sustain you through many trials and tribulations. You have to practice the fruits of the Spirit: love, joy, peace, kindness, goodness, peacefulness, faithfulness, gentleness and self-control (Galatians 5:22-23, NIV).

Prophets must seek GOD'S counsel over any and every form of manly counsel without engaging in rebellious actions. Prophets must seek GOD especially when speaking on HIS behalf because there are many deceptive spirits that sound like HIM, but are masked interrupters who intend to stop the spreading of the Gospel of JESUS CHRIST.

VIII.
Prophets and The Church

Prophets in the Bible rarely served in one church. Nor did any apostle. The prophet's ministry assignment was what many consider to be *itinerant* in this day and age. Prophets actually followed in JESUS' footsteps more than other five-fold ministers because they are builders. They traveled to places where the people needed them and encouraged them with the Word of The LORD. While true prophets should not try to be JESUS they walk by faith in declaring the Word of The LORD. Often, The LORD will move them from place to place to do so.

Over the years of my personal prophetic and apostolic development, I have learned that there is a difference between a Kingdom prophet and a Church prophet. It became evident nearly two decades ago when the prominence of prophets arose, that they would be labeled rebellious especially if they were not a consistent member and attendee of one church. GOD revealed to me that the true prophets would be persecuted for flowing with HIS Spirit and for traveling to different borders to speak on HIS behalf. The job of the adversary is to shut the mouths of the prophetic voices.

Now in the 21st century, you see more and more individuals claiming to be a prophet because what they have spoken has come to pass. As students of the Bible we should recall that GOD said HIS Word would not return to HIM void. Many gifts are in operation and with no repentance. It seems that those who have no prophetic foundation, development or mentorship are regarded as a mouthpiece of GOD just because they are speaking about what The LORD says and individuals are gravitating to them.

Words can come to pass when individuals believe that they will by faith, but when you are truly connected to GOD you will ask HIM to allow what HE wants to come to pass, into your life. That is the distinct difference between one who is yielded to GOD and desires a relationship with HIM, versus one who has not put in any effort to get to know about GOD but wants the benefits that HE gives.

When any leader in the five-fold ministry is totally yielded to GOD, their mistakes will lessen. There is a spirit of conviction that enters your life when you truly want more of GOD. Any apostle, prophet, evangelist, pastor or teacher should surrender to GOD first before releasing anything on HIS behalf. When GOD shares something with you, pray before releasing a word because a test of your loyalty to GOD will always follow. Prophets are often labeled rebellious, misinformed or immature when they release what others do not care to hear. Therefore, the test of loyalty to GOD comes in whether he or she will be deceptive in the message that is relayed.

Many prophets are only sharing prosperity messages and no words of warning. This is why much destruction has hit the church. Many prophets are not trained in a church before they are sent out to travel and minister. There must be some form of schooling that contributes to their prophetic development. In the nonspiritual world, some people drop out of school and go on to be successful. They have a level of education even if they received it at a very young age or for a short amount of time. This is a law of our land.

I am not implying that prophets cannot be trained without being a member of a church because The Holy Spirit is in fact a teacher, but one must know that they are hearing the voice of GOD. They must be taught the unadulterated Word of GOD by a yielded, Holy Spirit filled leader. This is absolutely vital to a prophet's survival in the prophetic ministry because the voice of ego or *self* can mimic the voice of GOD well before the enemy steps in to divert the prophet's path.

It is important to know the difference between a Kingdom of GOD prophet and a Church prophet.

Detrimental circumstances will transpire in churches that do not promote and teach about GOD. Incorrect teachings will taint any prophet or five-fold minister. We have witnessed individuals on platforms and while they claim to speak life into others, they esteem money and material things and not a true relationship with The LORD.

The spirit of prophecy's intent is to draw people to JESUS CHRIST (Revelation 19:10, NLT). GOD created prophets with the ultimate goal of drawing people to HIM, not to the prophet. In example, the Ethiopian eunuch's interaction with a messenger from GOD, introduced him to JESUS (Acts 8:27). Prophets, there are many people prophesying and proclaiming the works of The LORD but they are not prophets. You must be sure of who you are.

Acts chapter 2 gives an account of Apostle Peter teaching the people at Pentecost that Prophet Joel declared that GOD will pour HIS Spirit out on all people and that they would prophesy. When measuring the effectiveness of the prophetic word what must be determined is if the individuals that release the word are recipients of HIS Spirit to do HIS Will as prophets, or more concerned with their own personal will. Discern, pray and speak only as GOD permits you to.

When you are called as a Kingdom of GOD prophet, your mindset shifts from carnality to spirituality. You have an intimate relationship with GOD. Spirituality cannot really be seen, but it can be felt. Scripture says that "we walk by faith and not by sight" (2 Corinthians 5:7, KJV). A great deal of what we see happening on Earth is not comparable to what occurs in Heaven. This is why GOD moves speedily on the behalf of HIS Kingdom prophet. This type of prophet is quick to speak by faith and not be moved by what he or she sees. They hold on to the hem of JESUS' garment and never let go. Their complaints lessen and they do not throw in the towel regardless of what they go through.

People of the faith will question the prophet's conviction and label him or her as brainwashed or lost, nevertheless, a Kingdom prophet does not let go of GOD'S Hand. Scripture tells us that "without faith it is impossible to please GOD because anyone who comes to HIM must believe that HE exists and that HE rewards those that sincerely seek HIM" -Hebrews 11:6, NLT.

This is one of the most important principles that a Kingdom of GOD prophet must follow and adhere to. A Kingdom prophet should love GOD'S Church and never seek or intend to destroy it. They are builders, just as apostles are builders of The Body of CHRIST. They are to respect the Bride of CHRIST, yet not bow down to the laws of man that intend to replace the voice of GOD.

"So then you are no longer strangers and aliens but you are fellow citizens with the saints and members of the household of GOD, built on the foundation of the apostles and prophets, CHRIST JESUS himself being the cornerstone, in whom the whole structure, being joined together, grows into a holy temple in The LORD. In HIM you also are being built together into a dwelling place for GOD by The Spirit" Ephesians 2:19-22, ESV.

A church prophet must be planted in a place of spiritual development; a place where their gift is not muffled. They must be a member of a church where the prophetic is welcomed and regarded as the voice of GOD. They should be a member of a church where they are constantly developed and not just in prophetic language (i.e. "The LORD says"). They must be trained in prayer strategies and faith.

The church itself is prophetic and should acknowledge and adhere to the prophetic voice of GOD. In the church there should be diversities of gifts because we are many gifts that originate from One Spirit. When the prophet is in a church and are not permitted to operate in their spiritual gift, the Church will eventually decompose:

"Therefore my brothers, be eager to prophesy and do not forbid speaking in tongues" (1 Corinthians 14:39, KJV). If prophecy is not permitted, the church will not survive, so there is a need for the church prophet. They just cannot be suffocated and boxed in. At the same time, they must be humble and learn how to deal with the adversarial attacks that will try to discredit their assignment to GOD.

Some people will know that you are a prophet but will try to give you another position in the church that deviates you from the call on your life. You will have to learn how to walk in love as it is described in 1 Corinthians 14: 1-5, NIV, because the church is expected to survive with the application of biblical teachings and the operation of GOD'S gifts:

"Follow the way of love and eagerly desire gifts of the Spirit, especially prophecy. For anyone who speaks in a tongue does not speak to people but to God. Indeed, no one understands them; they utter mysteries by the Spirit. But the one who prophesies speaks to people for their strengthening, encouraging and comfort. Anyone who speaks in a tongue edifies themselves, but the one who prophesies edifies the church. I would like every one of you to speak in tongues, but I would rather have you prophesy. The one who prophesies is greater than the one who speaks in tongues, unless someone interprets, so that the church may be edified."

The church has to be a place where prophets can be developed and not attacked because of their gifting. If the church is not prophetic then how can believers of GOD impact the world? There should be no quarrels between the apostles and prophets because it interrupts a pure, holy fulfillment and occupancy of the Spirit of GOD in that physical and spiritual space called *Church*.

Kingdom of GOD prophets acknowledge that they are to impact the world and are often dismissed from the local church. They usually see things the way that GOD views them. When churches are operating out of order prophets have a difficult time dealing with those who allow this behavior.

There must be a positive cohesiveness amongst the leaders of the church and the prophet who is a member of the church. JESUS CHRIST must be the center of their ministry and their goal must be to win souls for GOD and HIS Kingdom. Leaders in the church must allow the prophetic gift to breathe again.

GOD desires for more souls to join HIS Kingdom and some people will not believe in GOD nor build a relationship with HIM until they see a positive ministry collaboration amongst the five-fold ministers. The prophet must be included and regarded for they are GOD'S voice to the Church.

"Lay not up for yourselves treasures upon earth; where moth and dust doth corrupt, and where thieves break through and steal: But lay up for yourselves treasures in heaven, where neither moth nor rust doth corrupt, and where thieves do not break through nor steal"- Matthew 6:19-20, KJV.

IX.
Prophetic Prayer

Prayer is the foundation and establishment of a true prophet's ministry. Prayer atones one with GOD and for the prophet to be used by GOD, there must be continual communication between the both of them. The ministry that we have been entrusted with should be reflective of our relationship with GOD. It is impossible to speak as HIS mouthpiece without clarity and directives from HIM.

Prophets are not only to pray for themselves but for others. They are to pray that the Will of The LORD be done and not their own. JESUS the Chief Prophet, demonstrated to HIS followers what a relationship with GOD looks like. JESUS did not heal others and perform miracles because HE was GOD in the flesh, HE performed miracles because HE depended on HIS Heavenly Father.

Prophetic prayer is simply speaking the Word of GOD into existence by faith. It is a way of reminding GOD that "It has been written that man shall live not by bread alone" (Matthew 4:4, KJV) and that we are to be completely dependent on HIM. This is why there are some Kingdom prophets. They do not rely on the world's systems because they work for JESUS CHRIST. When you are chosen to be a prophet you have to live in the world yet be balanced and realistic enough not to be overwhelmed by it. You are to consider the

Kingdom of GOD in every decision that you make. While you have your own personal needs, you have to include GOD in everything that you do.

This means that you will have to learn how to become fully reliant on GOD. You cannot exclude HIM from any part of your life because HE is always there anyway. But, HE wants to be invited into your life and wants to know that you need HIM. You will not be successful as a prophet if you do not rely on HIM for everything. HE will prosper you, but you have to believe that HE is the One that causes you to prosper.

You cannot serve two gods and you have to be willing to follow and serve GOD even when you do not see physical financial compensation. A prayer life will keep you humble and your attention will shift to the things that GOD wants instead of what you want.

Prophetic prayer should consist of repentance and restoration between the individual(s) and GOD. The purpose of prayer is to correct anything that we have done incorrectly in the sight of The LORD. We should never think that we are not sinners. To think that we do not do anything wrong is dishonest and deceitful. Our thoughts are not always the best, nor are our words or actions. We should continually seek GOD through prayer just to praise and worship HIM for forgiving us for the sins that we have committed. "If I had harbored sin in my heart, The LORD would not have listened"-Psalm 66:18, NET.

Prophets, maintain a strong, stable prayer life and repentant relationship with GOD. You have to share what HE is saying to the people when HE instructs you to do so, but you cannot steal HIS glory. At times you will not be required to deliver a message but you will need to intercede for others. We should not become so distracted with what everyone else is doing until we do not fulfill our assignment. No prophet is like another. We all have different callings in the prophetic and distinct expressions of our gifts.

Some of us are called to pray and declare what says The LORD during our times of intercession. You will not always have a microphone to hold. A large percentage of your time should be dedicated to praying, ministering to and encouraging The LORD through worship and fasting (Acts 13:2, NLT). This is what moves The HOLY SPIRT to speak to you and express what is to come.

Social media has provided us the opportunity to reach millions of people all over the world but prophets must be especially careful not to crossover into a realm of false prophecy. So is the same with traveling all over the world to minister; one must live holy and not excuse immoral behavior as an imperfection. GOD desires dependent, loyal and faithful prophets to help to heal the land.

Consistent communication with GOD will bring about a desire to live righteously for HIM. Our bodies should be a living sacrifice. Eventually HE will respond to your prayers and show you your faults especially when the heart is truly repentant. Prophet Daniel prayed for the exiled Jews: "We do not make requests of you because we are righteous, but because of your great mercy" Daniel 9:18-NIV. It is not our obedience that moved GOD to answer us, but HIS mercy towards us. GOD is calling the true prophets back to a place of fervent prayer and intercession. Not only will their outward appearance reflect a life of holiness but so will their spiritual being. The enemy has crept into the church unaware and impersonated the Kingdom, stripping the true prophets of their voice:

"Some ungodly people have wormed their way into your churches, saying that God's marvelous grace allows us to live immoral lives. The condemnation of such people was recorded long ago, for they have denied our only Master and Lord, Jesus Christ"- Jude 1:4 TLB.

The times that we are living in are the last days that scripture speaks of and we should depend on GOD to help us through everything that we deal with spiritually and naturally. We must depend on HIM to help us to save souls and to also help us to provide and care for our families. We should not have more concern for our daily activities than we have for GOD. Our ministries should not be elevated higher than HIM. Nor should the prophetic words of direction that HE shares with us.

Prophetic ministry can become an obsession if you do not have a strong prayer life or submissive lifestyle. I cannot stress this enough. Often in the budding stages of the prophetic, the prophet will become consumed with whether words come to pass instead of trusting that GOD will bring those words to pass, whether they receive a testimony or not. We must be careful not to endorse our ministries on testimonies alone. Our ministries are validated by GOD and true prophets must be confident in understanding and believing this.

Prophets, you must co-labor with JESUS CHRIST. You must believe in HIM, you must study HIS earthly life, and you must communicate with HIM often. This is the only way that your ministry assignment will be effective. Do not become consumed with the work until you forget who employs you. There are many prophets that are prophesying who do not believe in JESUS. Just because they sound good and just because they talk about GOD does not prove that they have a relationship with HIM, HIS Son or The Spirit.

"I have set you an example that you should do as I have done for you. Very truly I tell you, no servant is greater than his master, nor is a messenger greater than the one who sent him"- John 13:15-16, NIV.

X.
Reflection

True prophets are highly disregarded by those who do not fear GOD. In this day and age, many prophetic people are concerned with being promoted to apostleship, when they have yet to develop as a prophet. The functions of the five-fold ministry gifts have become comparable to job promotions in the secular workplace. If a person has served as a prophet for so many years, they may be deceived into believing that they have been promoted to apostleship. This notion is very far from the truth and GOD is not pleased with man's self-promotion into something as sacred as a ministry office. HE wants us to be pleased with having and operating in the most excellent gift- LOVE.

"Follow the way of love and eagerly desire gifts of the Spirit, especially prophecy"- 1 Corinthians 14:1, KJV.

When you operate in true agape love, the type of love that JESUS CHRIST has for us, GOD freely gives HIS Spiritual gifts to us. This is why Prophet Joel says "After this I will pour out My Spirit on all humanity; then your sons and daughters will prophesy, your old men will have dreams, and your young men will see visions"- Joel 2:28, HCSB. It is *after* release and restoration from the plagues of the enemy that entrapped many and destroyed the physical church, that GOD will share HIS Spirit with the people. We must take into account that the scriptures in The Book of Joel were written for us to enter into relationship with GOD and not deny HIS existence. Therefore, prophets should not be denied but welcomed as they prophesy in the midst of catastrophe because it takes a willing spirit and love for GOD to be able to do so.

Prophets must remember that sacrificial love is key and is not lead by friendship, sexual interactions or brotherly love. It can be difficult to separate our physical emotions from our spiritual assignment but it has to be done. We have to place the needs of others before ourselves when we are doing spiritual work. We cannot be selfish. We are not to glamourize our gifts or our lives. Surely, GOD will prosper us for walking in obedience, but never show off. It conveys a message that we think that we are better than or more blessed than others. We should never falsely "brag" on GOD because we will be ridiculed not only by people but more importantly by GOD (Matthew 12:36-37, NIV).

Since the prophetic became more prominent in the late 1980's we have seen many who claimed to be prophets come and go. Prophets must not allow money to determine what their mouth releases. If you want to survive naturally and spiritually do not minister for dishonest gain: "Feed the flock of GOD;

care for it willingly, not grudgingly; not for what you will be able to get out of it" 1 Peter 5:2, NIV. Do not hold ministry meetings to make others jealous because GOD is not glorified in that. Your goal should be to lay down your life for the Gospel.

Serving in ministry is challenging because GOD is dealing with our character flaws as we develop into mature believers. Serving in the prophetic ministry is even more difficult. You have to be sure not to strive for recognition because GOD will only make your name great when HE is ready. Popularity on earth does not mean that your name is respected by GOD. On the other hand, you may be favored by GOD, but in order to survive as a true prophet, you cannot be concerned with public attention or accolades.

Philippians 2 teaches us that JESUS made Himself of no reputation.

If you want to be fruitful in the prophetic ministry you must know who you are. Then you must learn how to be content with who GOD says that you are. You have to lay aside your personal hurts and fears to effectively obey and serve GOD. You will not always feel comfortable, you will be denied, your character will be attacked but scripture provides this assurance:

"If you are insulted because of the name of CHRIST you are blessed because the SPIRIT of glory- the SPIRIT of GOD- is resting on you" (1 Peter 4:14, GW).

PRAYER

Father, we believe in our hearts and confess with our mouths that JESUS is our Messiah. We willingly confess our sins, transgressions and shortcomings that have caused us to fall short of Your glory. Protect us as You have chosen us to fulfill Your prophetic ministry here on Earth. Let no emptiness be found in us. Your Spirit fills the weak areas of our lives with Your strength and might. Let every word, thought or action that has built walls between us and be forgiven as we offer our repentance to You.

We confess that You are our all sufficient One in every area of our lives. We ask You by Your authority to protect us your mouthpieces and keep us accountable as we complete Your work. Cause us to seek You in every area of our lives. Fill us with your Ruach Spirit and help us to understand your commands. Let our prayers and worship bring glory to You. Show us dreams and visions as we serve as earthly architects for the Body of CHRIST. We are builders and depend on Your blueprint. Help us to learn more about You and Your glory, for this is the only way that we can survive in this earth realm. We cannot depend on man to save us for You are our Savior. Help us to willingly seek the Kingdom of GOD above all else and live righteously, we know that in doing this that You will give us everything that we need. We thank you for provision as we seek Your Kingdom and all that is right. We will not bow down to foreign gods.

Father, command your intercessors and Kingdom guardians to stand garrison around us Your chosen vessels and protect us from warfare assigned from the places that try to exalt itself against You and steal Your glory. Favor us in all that we do and protect us as we speak against the works of the enemy. Deal with us in the Spirit realm and show us divine methods and strategies to defeat the kingdom of darkness. Help us to handle our assignment in the Spirit so that we will set order according to your commands. Let our words be reflective of life and help us to look beyond our personal feelings and emotions as we serve Your people so that You can be glorified.

Provide us with divine insight to defeat the attacks of struggle and envy as we serve in the prophetic ministry. Help us to be obedient to You and respectful to others. We vow to represent Your Kingdom with excellence and refuse to bicker with others or fall to the attacks of carnality. We depend on the Spirit of GOD to bring scripture to our remembrance as we deal with all matters and we adhere to 2 Timothy 2:14 which instructs us to "not quarrel and fight over words because such arguments do not benefit those who hear them."

We command every satanic agent to leave our presence and our lives. We bring the Blood of JESUS between us and we cover our lives, thoughts, emotions, hearts and minds with the Blood of JESUS. Thank You Father that You send confusion into the camps of the enemy and that we are impenetrable and not approachable as we walk the straight and narrow path that You have set before us. We submit every area of our lives to you so that no deception, contamination or perversion can interrupt our assignments.

We willingly pray this prayer to You in the Name of JESUS so that we will continue to prosper in all that works that You give our hands to do. Help us to obey Your voice and to abide in You. John 15 teaches us that in order to have relationship with You that we must produce fruit. Continue to prune us and develop our character so that we can bring glory to You. As prophets we must remain in You and we ask You to hold on to us and keep us from straying or wavering. Build us up in our most holy faith.

We lay aside every weight that has come to test our faith and we will fight the good fight of faith. We will teach those who You entrust us with to war for their prophecies through prayer and fasting. We will fast and pray regularly and not become consumed with what the world is doing. We want to develop accountable relationships with You and remain faithful to the covenant that You made with us. We ask You to keep us covered and protect us with the Ruach of GOD. Restore us and help us to recognize our faults through repentance when we do those things that are not pleasing to You. We pray for those who we will encounter that their lives will be transformed because of the Gospel of JESUS CHRIST and not because of us. Teach us true humility and keep Your Kingdom at the forefront of our thoughts and motives as we serve You.

We understand that there is an arising of prophets that are forthcoming and we ask you to alleviate the spirit of competition and jealousy that is assigned from the adversary to deter the promotion of Your Kingdom. Encourage us to support one another and to respect the different operations of the five-fold ministry gifts. Help us to embrace our uniqueness and to demonstrate our total trust and true spirit of collaboration in You as we minister to the nations.

We thank You that You are our Advocate and we are grateful that You have chosen us to work along with The HOLY SPIRIT and prepare others for the return of JESUS CHRIST. Help us to be more accountable and fearful of You. May Your name be glorified in every thought, action, and work that You allow us to do. Lead us and guide us to complete the prophetic work that will only bring glory to Your name.

Thank You for entrusting us to speak as You speak and to heal the land that You have blessed us to occupy. We cover our land with prophetic decrees and declarations that we will be restored and that Your Spirit will rest upon all of Your people as they come into the knowledge of Your Kingdom. LORD, speak to us, for we are listening, speak to us prophetically so that your Church can be saved. In The Name of JESUS. Amen.

Prophet, be strong, willingly learn through trial and error, and avoid being stuck in bondage. None of our earthly vessels are perfect but GOD chose you so that you can be perfected by HIS grace and mercy. Do not elevate what has happened in your life above the plans that HE has for your life. SOAR!

"I consider that our present sufferings are not worth comparing with the glory that will be revealed in us" Romans 8:18-NIV.

You have to believe that your suffering is for a greater cause in order to successfully serve The LORD.

ABOUT

Iris L. Jones is a mother of two adult children, a five-fold minister and an employee of the educational government. She has over 16 years of experience in prophetic development and training and travels frequently to minister to and train others in prophetic ministry.

She is the Apostolic Prophetic overseer of Kingdom Ministries of Wisdom, a subsidiary of Iris L. Jones Enterprises, Inc. Iris is also an author and has written six books over the course of a seven-year period. She is a mentor to many, a sister to 8 siblings, a loyal friend and diligent witness of our Lord and Savior JESUS CHRIST.

In 2017, The Apostles & Prophets Institute was birthed through Iris L. Jones Ministries. This charge from GOD was for Iris to teach and equip Apostles and Prophets the basics for a successful ministry. The courses offered in an online setting, are scripture based and the teachings are relevant to the ministry and teachings of JESUS CHRIST.

For more information about Iris and the ministry that GOD has entrusted her with, please visit www.IRISLJONES.org.

Books Written by Iris L. Jones

One Simple Principle: I Will Give You the Keys to the Kingdom of Heaven- The Journey: Returning to Your Foundation in God" (Released April 2011)

Witty Sayings for the Winning Soul (Released September 2011)

Effective Prayers That Avail Much (Released September 2012)

Effective Warfare Prayers That Avail Much (Released February 2013)

Affirmations that Move the Throne Room of GOD (Released January 2014)

Please visit www.IRISLJONES.org to purchase these books.

Love GOD. Love HIS People. Serve GOD. Serve HIS World.

www.ingramcontent.com/pod-product-compliance
Lightning Source LLC
Chambersburg PA
CBHW042303150426
43196CB00005B/62